TAPPING SCRIPTS FOR HEALING, ATTRACTING, AND FINDING LOVE

EFT for Positive Living

Christa Smith

Special thanks to the participants of my workshops, tapping circles and clients from which these tapping scripts were inspired.

Satisfying relationships don't bring alignment. Alignment brings satisfying relationships. Do you see what must come first?

ABRAHAM-HICKS

CONTENTS

Title Page

Copyright

Dedication

Epigraph

Introduction   1

What is EFT?   3

How Does EFT Help With Relationship Issues?   4

How to Do EFT Tapping   5

Tapping Tips   9

How to Use These Scripts   11

Tapping Scripts   13

I Feel Unworthy of Love   14

There is No One Out There For Me   17

I Sabotage My Relationships   20

I Reject Anyone Who Loves Me   23

I Always Pick the Wrong Partner   26

I Don't Know How to Make a Relationship Work   29

I Can't Be Happy Until I'm In a Relationship   32

My Expectations Are Too High   35

I'm Too Damaged to Love Again   38

I Have a Broken Heart   41

I Have a Bad Track Record   44

I Have a Fear of Abandonment   47

I Have a Fear of Intimacy   50

I Have a Fear of Rejection   53

I Have a Fear of Betrayal   56

I'm Afraid of Being Controlled   59

I'm Afraid of Losing My Independence   62

I'm Afraid I Will Always Be Alone   65

I'm Afraid to Commit to a Relationship   68

I'm Too Busy For a Relationship   71

I'm Too Insecure   74

I'm Too Needy   77

I'm Too Shy   80

I Feel Unattractive   83

It is Not Safe For Anyone to Love Me   86

It is Not Safe For Me to Love Someone   89

About The Author   93

Books By This Author   95

INTRODUCTION

Welcome to EFT for Positive Living: Tapping Scripts for Healing, Attracting, and Finding Love!

This book was inspired by my clients and workshop attendees who voiced their frustration about not knowing what to say when tapping on their own. If you are like them, and find it challenging to formulate set-up statements and reminder phrases, this book is for you! The EFT for Positive Living books have been designed to take the guesswork out of tapping and will assist you in making the process much easier.

If you are new to EFT, I highly recommend reading The EFT Manual by Dawson Church or The Tapping Solution by Nick Ortner to get a better understanding of EFT and how it works, or visit my website at www.Christa-Smith.com.

Since there are many aspects involved around the topic of relationships, such as emotions, beliefs, and memories, it is impossible to address them all in this book. I have included here some of the most common.

For each of these aspects I have created two tapping scripts:

1) The first script flows as if you were having a conversation with yourself or speaking to a friend. It taps out the negative thoughts, beliefs and emotions you may be experiencing around the aspect and then taps in the positive ones.

2) The second script is inspired by Patricia Carrington's Choices Method and helps to solidify the changes you want to make. Use this technique after the intensity of the issue has been signifi-

cantly decreased.

Keep in mind that these scripts are only a guide. Feel free to add, omit, or replace words to fit your situation.

WHAT IS EFT?

EFT (Emotional Freedom Technique) is a form of psychological acupressure based on the ancient principles of acupuncture. Instead of needles, EFT combines gentle tapping on key acupuncture points while focusing your thoughts on pain, uncomfortable emotions, memories, cravings or any other problem. EFT is a complementary therapy that helps the body to re-balance itself, and accelerates healing.

An energy imbalance in the body can cause effects such as illness, physical pain, depression, anxiety, fear, anger, etc. EFT balances the energy system and helps to relieve psychological stress and physical pain. Restoring the balance of the energy system allows the body and mind to resume their natural healing abilities. EFT often works when nothing else will.

EFT is easy to learn and apply. While focusing on an issue you want to release, affirmation and reminder phrases are repeated while tapping various acupressure points on the body with your fingers. Often the process only takes minutes to achieve results. In other cases it may take a little longer if there are underlying issues that also need to be addressed.

HOW DOES EFT HELP WITH RELATIONSHIP ISSUES?

The interaction we have with others plays a huge role in influencing our beliefs about ourselves and the world around us. If the relationships in your past have been less than positive, your subconscious mind may be holding on to the negative emotions to protect you from being hurt again. Feelings such as fear and self-doubt are major roadblocks to having loving, fulfilling relationships. If you want to move forward and attract a loving partner, you must release these emotional blocks. EFT tapping is the perfect tool to assist you.

EFT tapping can help you neutralize painful memories, change habits and patterns of behavior, release limiting beliefs that keep you stuck, dissolve past influences that contribute to failed relationships (such as traumas and fears), and improve self image.

EFT tapping is a simple yet powerful technique that can be used for relationship issues and any other area of your life that needs improvement or change.

HOW TO DO EFT TAPPING

The following explains the basic steps:

1. Identify the Emotion or Issue

All you do here is make a mental note of what is bothering you. This will be your focal point while you're tapping. Examples might be: I don't have enough money, my brother embarrassing me at my 9th birthday party or having doubts about your ability to attract a soul mate. Be sure you are only targeting one issue at a time. Trying to combine issues will compromise your results.

2. Establish the Initial Intensity

Before you begin tapping, establish a before level of the issue's intensity by assigning a number to it on a scale from 0-10, where 10 is the worst the issue has ever been and 0 is no problem at all. This serves as a benchmark so you can compare your progress after each tapping round. If, for example, you start at a 9 and eventually reach a 4, then you know you have achieved improvement.

Here are some useful methods to help you access your issue(s) and arrive at your 0-10 numbers.

> For emotional issues, you can recreate the memories in your mind and assess their discomforts.

> For physical ailments you can simply assess the existing pain or

discomfort.

3. The Setup

The Setup is a process used to start each round of tapping. By designing a simple phrase and saying it while continuously tapping the karate chop (KC) point, you let your system know what you're trying to address.

When designing this phrase there are two goals to achieve:

1) Acknowledging the issue.
2) Accepting yourself despite the problem.

The common setup phrase is: "Even though I have this [issue or problem], I deeply and completely accept myself."

For example:

This sore shoulder:

"Even though I have this sore shoulder, I deeply and completely accept myself."

This fear of heights:

"Even though I have this fear of heights, I deeply and completely accept myself."

This humiliation at my eighth grade graduation:

"Even though I have this humiliation at my eighth grade graduation, I deeply and completely accept myself."

You can use some flexibility when designing your Setup phrase. For example, instead of "this sore shoulder" you could say "Even though my shoulder hurts, I deeply and completely accept myself".

4. EFT Tapping Sequence

The EFT tapping sequence is tapping on the ends of nine meridian points that mirror each side of the body:

Tapping on these points stimulates and balances the body's energy pathways. To perform it, you tap each of the points shown in the diagram while saying a Reminder Phrase that keeps you tuned into the issue.

Eyebrow (EB): This point is at the inside edge of the eyebrow, above the inside corner of the eye.

Side of the Eye (SE): This point is on the bone bordering the outside corner of the eye.

Under the Eye (UE): This point is on the bone under the eye.

Under the Nose (UN): This point is in the indentation just between the middle of the nose and the middle of the upper lip.

Chin (CH): This point is on the middle of the chin, just below the crease.

Collarbone (CB): This point is at the end of the collar bone, next to the u-shaped indentation below the neck.

Under the Arm (UA): This point is in the area on the side of the chest about four inches below the armpit.

Top of the Head (TH): This point is at the crown of the head.

The Reminder Phrase is simple as you only need to identify the issue with some brief wording. Depending on your issue, you might say the following at each tapping point....

"This sore shoulder",

"This fear of heights",

"This humiliation at my eight grade graduation."

5. Test the Final Intensity

After tapping through the sequence of points, take a deep breath and re-check the intensity level. Evaluate an "after" level of the issue's intensity by assigning a number to it on a 0-10 scale. You compare this with the before level to see how much progress you have made. If you are not down to zero then repeat the process until you either achieve zero or plateau at some level.

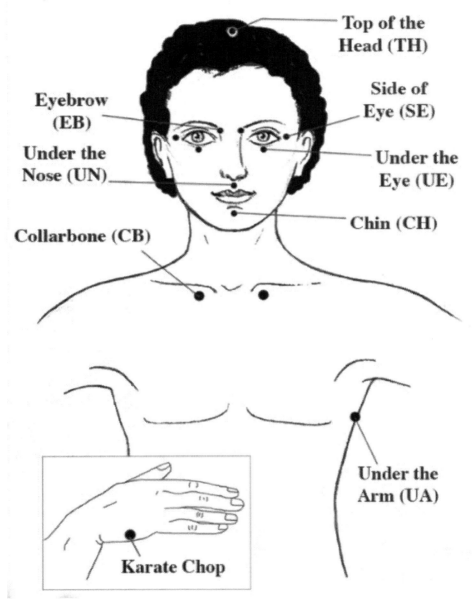

TAPPING TIPS

> You can use either hand, or both hands, and tap on either side of the body. Bilateral tapping (tapping on both sides of the body at once) may decrease the amount of time it takes to resolve an issue because you are sending the maximum amount of energy down through your body on both sides to reach wherever the blockages are.

> Use enough pressure when tapping to stimulate the meridians but not enough to hurt yourself. Use the same amount of pressure you would use if you were drumming your fingers on a table.

> Drink water before and after a tapping session. Water is a conductor of energy and can help get your energy flowing. It also helps to flush out any toxins that might be released from the tapping.

> Take a slow deep breath after tapping to help move the energy through your body.

> Yawning during tapping is a sign that you are releasing energy.

> Be persistent. If your intensity level is not releasing to a 0, keep tapping on the issue. You may need to use different wording, or there may be other aspects to address.

> Connect to your feelings. Be aware of your response to the thought or event you are thinking about.

> Be Specific. Rather than using general statements, try to focus on specific incidents. Or if it is pain in the body, describe the pain. Where is it?

> Tune in to your emotions. Say your statements and reminder phrases as though you mean them.

> If you're not making progress on an issue and you seem to be stuck, shout out the words. Really put emphasis on them and give them some ummph! Use swear words if you feel it will emphasize the feelings you are experiencing.

> If you are in a situation where you want to tap, but you're around other people and it does not feel appropriate to start tapping on yourself and repeating phrases, you can tap mentally. Simply imagine tapping on yourself for the current issue.

> Sometimes it might be necessary to change physical position, such as from sitting to standing, or even move to a different room.

> If an issue is not reducing, try tapping with a friend or relative if you are not able to work with an EFT practitioner. The positive intention and combined energy of two people can sometimes make the difference in releasing stubborn issues or problems.

> Try EFT tapping on everything! It only takes a few minutes and can change your life!

HOW TO USE THESE SCRIPTS

I am an advocate of positive thinking, but sometimes in order for change to occur, negative thinking needs to be acknowledged and addressed. For your subconscious mind to accept any changes, it is important to take an honest look at your limiting thoughts and beliefs, acknowledge them and be open to letting them go. These scripts are designed to assist in that process.

To begin, choose one of the scripts listed in the table of contents that pertains to you and triggers an emotional response. The tapping points have been added in front of each statement to simplify the process. Follow the tapping protocol and read the script of the aspect you are focusing on.

Before you begin tapping, find a quiet place where you can close your eyes and tune in to your thoughts. Take a deep breath and follow each script as a guide. Feel free to omit, add, or replace any statements to better suit your situation.

Start with the first script.

Round 1: Tap it out. Acknowledge the problem and the emotions that come with it. If you need more than one round to do this, repeat the phrases or add your own.

Round 2: What do you want? Prepare your subconscious mind for change. You are letting it know that there are alternatives and you are open to new possibilities.

Round 3: Tap it in. Your feelings and the way you react to circumstances is always a choice. In this round you will "tap in" your new choices.

After completing the tapping rounds, take a deep breath and tune in to the problem again. Do you feel better? If not, repeat the tapping sequence until you feel relief.

When you are feeling better about the problem, move on to the second script (Choices Method) to solidify the change. I recommend repeating these statements daily to help maintain your feeling of relief.

TAPPING SCRIPTS

I FEEL UNWORTHY
OF LOVE

Karate Chop: Even though I feel unworthy of love, I choose to accept myself anyway.

Karate Chop: Even though I don't feel worthy of love, I choose to accept myself anyway.

Karate Chop: Even though I feel like I don't deserve love, I choose to accept myself anyway.

Round 1:

Eyebrow: I feel unworthy of love

Side of Eye: I do not deserve to be loved

Under Eye: I don't know how someone could love me

Under Nose: I feel so unlovable

Chin: I have so many problems

Collarbone: I have too many flaws

Under Arm: I have too many challenges

Top of Head: I feel like I don't deserve love

Round 2:

Eyebrow: Maybe love is not for me

Side of Eye: Or maybe I'm scared of being rejected

Under Eye: Maybe I'm scared of being hurt

Under Nose: What if these beliefs come from my past?

Chin: What if I accepted this as truth from others?

Collarbone: What if I am worthy of love?

Under Arm: What if someone could love me as I am?

Top of Head: What if someone could accept me as I am?

Round 3:

Eyebrow: I'm ready to change these beliefs

Side of Eye: No one is perfect

Under Eye: We all have imperfections

Under Nose: Everyone deserves to be loved any way

Chin: I choose to accept my worthiness

Collarbone: I choose to allow myself to feel worthy of love

Under Arm: I choose to believe I deserve to be loved

Top of Head: I choose to start by loving myself unconditionally

When your intensity level is below a 2, move on to the following script:

I Feel Unworthy of Love

Karate Chop 3 Times:

Even though I feel unworthy of love, I choose to let go of this belief and accept my worthiness.

Round 1 (tapping through each point):

Even though I feel unworthy of love

Round 2 (tapping through each point):

I choose to let go of this belief and accept my worthiness

Round 3 (alternate while tapping through each point):

Even though I feel unworthy of love

I choose to let go of this belief and accept my worthiness

THERE IS NO ONE OUT THERE FOR ME

Karate Chop: Even though there is no one out there for me, I choose to love and accept myself anyway.

Karate Chop: Even though I feel like no one is compatible, I choose to love and accept myself anyway.

Karate Chop: Even though I don't think my soul mate exists, I choose to love and accept myself anyway.

Round 1:

Eyebrow: There is no one out there for me

Side of Eye: I've been hoping and looking

Under Eye: But haven't found them yet

Under Nose: I feel so incomplete

Chin: I feel so alone

Collarbone: I can't find someone who's compatible

Under Arm: I don't think my match exists

Top of Head: I doubt I'll ever find a soul mate

Round 2:

Eyebrow: I don't want to give up

Side of Eye: Maybe they're out there somewhere

Under Eye: Maybe they're looking for me

Under Nose: Maybe they can't find me

Chin: Because I keep pushing them away with my negativity

Collarbone: Maybe I can stay positive and optimistic

Under Arm: While living and loving my life as it is

Top of Head: Maybe I can be happy anyway

Round 3:

Eyebrow: I choose to believe there is someone out there for me

Side of Eye: I choose to believe I can attract my soul mate

Under Eye: In the meantime, I choose to be happy anyway

Under Nose: I choose to be be positive and optimistic

Chin: I choose to be the best person I can be

Collarbone: I choose to embrace my life as it is

Under Arm: I choose to love myself and be the partner I am looking for

Top of Head: I choose to believe the right person will come along at the perfect time

When your intensity level is below a 2, move on to the following script:

There is No One Out There For Me

Karate Chop 3 Times:

Even though there is no one out there for me, I choose to believe the right person will come along at the perfect time.

Round 1 (tapping through each point):

Even though there is no one out there for me

Round 2 (tapping through each point):

I choose to believe the right person will come along at the perfect time

Round 3 (alternate while tapping through each point):

Even though there is no one out there for me

I choose to believe the right person will come along at the perfect time

I SABOTAGE MY RELATIONSHIPS

Karate Chop: Even though I sabotage my relationships, I choose to love and accept myself anyway.

Karate Chop: Even though I have a pattern of self-sabotage in my relationships, I choose to love and accept myself anyway.

Karate Chop: Even though I tend to reject loving relationships, I choose to love and accept myself anyway.

Round 1:

Eyebrow: I tend to sabotage my relationships

Side of Eye: It's become a pattern

Under Eye: As soon as my partner starts to get too close

Under Nose: I begin to feel uncomfortable

Chin: I can always find an excuse to reject them

Collarbone: They don't meet my expectations

Under Arm: Either they have personality flaws

Top of Head: Or they can't be trusted

Round 2:

Eyebrow: I want to have a healthy, loving relationship

Side of Eye: But the truth is I don't feel worthy or deserving

Under Eye: My past has caused so much internal conflict

Under Nose: I want to change these misguided behaviors of sabotage

Chin: I want to feel deserving of lasting love

Collarbone: I want to feel worthy and confident

Under Arm: I want to learn to trust myself and others

Top of Head: I want to feel valued for who I am

Round 3:

Eyebrow: I now choose to end this self-sabotaging behavior

Side of Eye: I now choose to let my past go by loving it

Under Eye: I choose to open my heart and allow myself to heal

Under Nose: I choose to release unrealistic expectations

Chin: I choose to believe that I am worthy of love

Collarbone: I choose to believe I can have a loving relationship

Under Arm: I choose to honor and value the person I am

Top of Head: I choose to be open to loving someone and being loved

When your intensity level is below a 2, move on to the following script:

I Sabotage My Relationships

Karate Chop 3 Times:

Even though I sabotage my relationships, I choose to end this self-sabotaging behavior and believe I am worthy of love.

Round 1 (tapping through each point):

Even though I sabotage my relationships

Round 2 (tapping through each point):

I choose to end this self-sabotaging behavior and believe I am worthy of love

Round 3 (alternate while tapping through each point):

Even though I sabotage my relationships

I choose to end this self-sabotaging behavior and believe I am worthy of love

I REJECT ANYONE WHO LOVES ME

Karate Chop: Even though I reject anyone that loves me, I choose to accept myself anyway.

Karate Chop: Even though I'm uncomfortable being loved, I choose to accept myself anyway.

Karate Chop: Even though I don't like getting close to anyone, I choose to accept myself anyway.

Round 1:

Eyebrow: I tend to reject anyone who loves me

Side of Eye: I don't like getting close to anyone

Under Eye: I feel uncomfortable being loved

Under Nose: I feeling uncomfortable giving love

Chin: I push people away

Collarbone: I feel I have to protect myself

Under Arm: I have built walls around me

Top of Head: I have to keep my guard up

Round 2:

Eyebrow: I don't know why I do this

Side of Eye: Maybe I'm afraid of being hurt

Under Eye: Maybe I'm afraid of rejection

Under Nose: I want to be able to open my heart

Chin: But I am so afraid

Collarbone: I want to release this fear

Under Arm: But I don't know how

Top of Head: I want to be open to love

Round 3:

Eyebrow: I now choose to release this fear

Side of Eye: I choose to begin by connecting with my higher power

Under Eye: I choose to go within to begin this healing

Under Nose: I choose to set the intention to be open to love

Chin: I choose to tear down this wall, one brick at a time

Collarbone: I choose to believe it is safe for me to love and be loved

Under Arm: I choose to be patient with myself

Top of Head: I choose to start by loving myself

When your intensity level is below a 2, move on to the following script:

I Reject Anyone Who Loves Me

Karate Chop 3 Times:

Even though I reject anyone that loves me, I choose to release this fear and begin by loving myself.

Round 1 (tapping through each point):

Even though I reject anyone that loves me

Round 2 (tapping through each point):

I choose to release this fear and begin by loving myself

Round 3 (alternate while tapping through each point):

Even though I reject anyone that loves me

I choose to release this fear and begin by loving myself

I ALWAYS PICK THE WRONG PARTNER

Karate Chop: Even though I always pick the wrong partner, I choose to love and accept myself anyway.

Karate Chop: Even though I pick partners who are not right for me, I choose to love and accept myself anyway.

Karate Chop: Even though I always make the wrong relationship choice, I choose to love and accept myself anyway.

Round 1:

Eyebrow: I have a pattern of picking the wrong partner

Side of Eye: I always pick the wrong men/women

Under Eye: I seem to have a broken "partner picker"

Under Nose: I make the same mistakes over and over

Chin: I choose men/women for the wrong reasons

Collarbone: It always leads to problems down the line

Under Arm: I have a history of failed relationships

Top of Head: I'm afraid I'll make another wrong choice

Round 2:

Eyebrow: I'm so ready to break this pattern

Side of Eye: I'm ready to make better choices

Under Eye: I want to get it right next time

Under Nose: There must be someone out there who is compatible

Chin: I want to choose someone for the right reasons

Collarbone: I want to be more aware of the red flags at the beginning

Under Arm: I want to find a lasting, loving relationship

Top of Head: I want to learn to trust my inner guidance

Round 3:

Eyebrow: I now choose to start listening my inner voice

Side of Eye: I choose to start trusting my gut feeling

Under Eye: I choose to be conscious of the messages my body gives me

Under Nose: I choose to take my time and not rush into anything

Chin: I choose to be gentle with myself and keep trying

Collarbone: I choose to get clear on what I want and set my intention to attract it

Under Arm: I choose to believe I can find Mr Right/Ms Right

Top of Head: I choose to be open to allowing the right partner to come into my life

When your intensity level is below a 2, move on to the following script:

I Always Pick the Wrong Partner

Karate Chop 3 Times:

Even though I always pick the wrong partner, I choose to start paying closer attention to the voice of my Inner Guidance.

Round 1 (tapping through each point):

Even though I always pick the wrong partner

Round 2 (tapping through each point):

I choose to start paying closer attention to the voice of my Inner Guidance

Round 3 (alternate while tapping through each point):

Even though I always pick the wrong partner

I choose to start paying closer attention to the voice of my Inner Guidance

I DON'T KNOW
HOW TO MAKE A
RELATIONSHIP WORK

Karate Chop: Even though I don't know how to make a relationship work, I choose to love and accept myself anyway.

Karate Chop: Even though I don't know how to make a relationship last, I choose to love and accept myself anyway.

Karate Chop: Even though I have failed at maintaining a relationship, I choose to love and accept myself anyway.

Round 1:

Eyebrow: I don't know how to make a relationship work

Side of Eye: I've failed miserably in the past

Under Eye: My relationships never last

Under Nose: I have had poor role models

Chin: So I just don't know how it's done

Collarbone: I don't have the confidence

Under Arm: And I don't have the know-how

Top of Head: I am at a loss to knowing how to make it work

Round 2:

Eyebrow: I really want to have a lasting relationship

Side of Eye: I want to fall in love and stay in love

Under Eye: I want to share my life with another person

Under Nose: I want to experience loving commitment

Chin: There are many happy couples out there

Collarbone: What if I can have that kind of love too?

Under Arm: I am smart enough to figure this out

Top of Head: Maybe the answers are within me

Round 3:

Eyebrow: I choose to believe it is possible for me to have lasting love

Side of Eye: I choose to believe that I can have a successful relationship

Under Eye: I've learned what I don't want

Under Nose: So I can create what I do want

Chin: I can take my time

Collarbone: And allow God/Spirit to guide me

Under Arm: I can start by loving myself

Top of Head: And open my heart to joyful possibilities

When your intensity level is below a 2, move on to the following script:

I Don't Know How to Make a Relationship Work

Karate Chop 3 Times:

Even though I don't know how to make a relationship work, I choose to start by loving myself and allow God/Spirit to guide me.

Round 1 (tapping through each point):

Even though I don't know how to make a relationship work

Round 2 (tapping through each point):

I choose to start by loving myself and allow God/Spirit to guide me

Round 3 (alternate while tapping through each point):

Even though I don't know how to make a relationship work

I choose to start by loving myself and allow God/Spirit to guide me

I CAN'T BE HAPPY UNTIL I'M IN A RELATIONSHIP

Karate Chop: Even though I can't be happy until I'm in a relationship, I accept myself and my feelings.

Karate Chop: Even though I need to be in a relationship before I can be happy, I accept myself and my feelings.

Karate Chop: Even though I can only be happy if I'm sharing my life with someone, I accept myself and my feelings.

Round 1:

Eyebrow: I feel so unhappy being single

Side of Eye: I long to be in a relationship

Under Eye: It's lonely being on my own

Under Nose: Happiness seems to elude me

Chin: I feel a need to be in a relationship

Collarbone: I want to share my life with someone

Under Arm: I can't seem to move past this

Top of Head: I feel like I can't be happy until I find a partner

Round 2:

Eyebrow: I want to be happy either way

Side of Eye: It would be awesome if I found someone

Under Eye: But I want to be happy on my own too

Under Nose: I wish I could shake this need for a relationship

Chin: I want to choose a partner out of love, not need

Collarbone: I want to experience happiness now

Under Arm: I want to have fun and enjoy my life

Top of Head: I want to love myself and be my own best friend

Round 3:

Eyebrow: I now choose to release this need for a relationship

Side of Eye: I choose to focus on what I do have

Under Eye: I choose to be happy with my life as it is now

Under Nose: I am open and ready for a wonderful relationship

Chin: But will no longer put my life on hold until he/she comes

Collarbone: I choose to love and live to the fullest

Under Arm: I choose to be free and joyful

Top of Head: I choose to find happiness in each and every day

When your intensity level is below a 2, move on to the following script:

I Can't Be Happy Until I'm In a Relationship

Karate Chop 3 Times:

Even though I can't be happy until I'm in a relationship, I choose to release this belief and embrace my life as it is now.

Round 1 (tapping through each point):

Even though I can't be happy until I'm in a relationship

Round 2 (tapping through each point):

I choose to release this belief and embrace my life as it is now

Round 3 (alternate while tapping through each point):

Even though I can't be happy until I'm in a relationship

I choose to release this belief and embrace my life as it is now

MY EXPECTATIONS ARE TOO HIGH

Karate Chop: Even though my expectations are too high, I deeply and completely accept myself.

Karate Chop: Even though I have very high expectations, I deeply and completely accept myself.

Karate Chop: Even though no one will ever meet my high expectations, I deeply and completely accept myself.

Round 1:

Eyebrow: I have high expectations

Side of Eye: Of what I want in a partner

Under Eye: Of what I want in a relationship

Under Nose: No one has been able to meet my expectations

Chin: I don't know if anyone ever will

Collarbone: I know I don't want to settle

Under Arm: I wonder if I need to be more realistic

Top of Head: I wonder if my expectations are unreasonable

Round 2:

Eyebrow: I just want to be happy

Side of Eye: I want to have a successful relationship

Under Eye: "Settling" is not an option for me

Under Nose: If my partner can't meet my checklist of requirements

Chin: I would rather be single

Collarbone: I may have high expectations

Under Arm: But it's better than setting them too low

Top of Head: I deserve to have a healthy, happy relationship

Round 3:

Eyebrow: I choose to hold on to my reasonable expectations

Side of Eye: I choose to hold out for a partner who is respectful and kind

Under Eye: I choose to hold out for a partner who shares my values

Under Nose: I choose to hold out for a partner who is emotionally available

Chin: I choose to hold out for a partner who is open and loving

Collarbone: These requests are more than reasonable

Under Arm: I choose to believe that my ideal partner exists

Top of Head: And will come into my life at the perfect time

When your intensity level is below a 2, move on to the following script:

My Expectations Are Too High

Karate Chop 3 Times:

Even though my expectations are too high, I choose to hold on to my reasonable expectations and believe my ideal partner exists.

Round 1 (tapping through each point):

Even though my expectations are too high

Round 2 (tapping through each point):

I choose to hold on to my reasonable expectations and believe my ideal partner exists

Round 3 (alternate while tapping through each point):

Even though my expectations are too high

I choose to hold on to my reasonable expectations and believe my ideal partner exists

I'M TOO DAMAGED
TO LOVE AGAIN

Karate Chop: Even though I'm too damaged to love again, I choose to accept myself anyway.

Karate Chop: Even though I am emotionally damaged, I choose to accept myself anyway.

Karate Chop: Even though I am damaged beyond repair, I choose to accept myself anyway.

Round 1:

Eyebrow: I'm too damaged to love again

Side of Eye: I'm emotionally wounded

Under Eye: The wounds run deep

Under Nose: I don't know if they will ever heal

Chin: My life has been a series of emotional trauma

Collarbone: I have suffered so much heartache

Under Arm: How will I ever recover?

Top of Head: I am damaged beyond repair

Round 2:

Eyebrow: I want to heal my emotional wounds

Side of Eye: I want to release the pain from the past

Under Eye: I want to feel emotionally healthy

Under Nose: I want to feel whole and complete

Chin: I want to love and be loved

Collarbone: Maybe I can recover from my past

Under Arm: Maybe there is hope for me yet

Top of Head: I may be damaged but I'm not doomed

Round 3:

Eyebrow: I now choose to give myself the time and space to heal

Side of Eye: I choose to see my past experiences as lessons for growth

Under Eye: I choose to reclaim my power and be strong again

Under Nose: I choose to open my heart to allow love to flow through me

Chin: I choose to believe I can be whole and complete

Collarbone: I choose to be hopeful for a healthier future

Under Arm: And someday when I'm ready

Top of Head: I choose to be open to a loving relationship

When your intensity level is below a 2, move on to the following script:

I'm Too Damaged to Love Again

Karate Chop 3 Times:

Even though I'm too damaged to love again, I choose to allow myself to heal and allow love to flow through me.

Round 1 (tapping through each point):

Even though I'm too damaged to love again

Round 2 (tapping through each point):

I choose to allow myself to heal and allow love to flow through me

Round 3 (alternate while tapping through each point):

Even though I'm too damaged to love again

I choose to allow myself to heal and allow love to flow through me

I HAVE A BROKEN HEART

Karate Chop: Even though I have a broken heart, I deeply and completely love and accept myself.

Karate Chop: Even though my heart is broken, I deeply and completely love and accept myself.

Karate Chop: Even though I am recovering from a broken heart, I deeply and completely love and accept myself.

Round 1:

Eyebrow: My heart is broken

Side of Eye: I'm having a hard time recovering

Under Eye: I have been deeply hurt

Under Nose: I feel like I'm in mourning

Chin: The pain sweeps through me

Collarbone: My heart just aches

Under Arm: I don't know if it will ever mend

Top of Head: I can't seem to get past the sadness

Round 2:

Eyebrow: I want to get through this

Side of Eye: I want to detach from the hurt

Under Eye: I want to release the pain

Under Nose: I want to release the grief

Chin: I want to fill the emptiness

Collarbone: I want to feel good again

Under Arm: I want to mend my heart

Top of Head: I want to move forward

Round 3:

Eyebrow: I choose to give myself time to mourn

Side of Eye: I choose to acknowledge the pain

Under Eye: I choose to surrender to it

Under Nose: I choose to have the courage to accept it

Chin: I choose to release the past and embrace the now

Collarbone: I choose to create a more joyful future

Under Arm: I choose to allow my heart to heal and be happy again

Top of Head: I choose to open my heart to love again

When your intensity level is below a 2, move on to the following script:

I Have a Broken Heart

Karate Chop 3 Times:

Even though I have a broken heart, I choose to release the pain and be open to a joyful future.

Round 1 (tapping through each point):

Even though I have a broken heart

Round 2 (tapping through each point):

I choose to release the pain and be open to a joyful future

Round 3 (alternate while tapping through each point):

Even though I have a broken heart

I choose to release the pain and be open to a joyful future

I HAVE A BAD TRACK RECORD

Karate Chop: Even though I have a bad track record, I am open to positive change.

Karate Chop: Even though my track record has not been good, I am open to positive change.

Karate Chop: Even though I have had a string of bad relationships, I am open to positive change.

Round 1:

Eyebrow: When it comes to relationships

Side of Eye: I have a bad track record

Under Eye: I've had a string of bad experiences

Under Nose: I tend to pick people who are not good for me

Chin: I dismiss my instincts

Collarbone: I ignore the red flags

Under Arm: And get involved anyway

Top of Head: I'm getting tired of striking out

Round 2:

Eyebrow: I'm ready to turn things around

Side of Eye: I want to have a healthy relationship

Under Eye: One that is characterized by respect

Under Nose: Where we trust and support each other

Chin: We share responsibility

Collarbone: We communicate openly and truthfully

Under Arm: There is negotiation and fairness

Top of Head: Where we are both equal

Round 3:

Eyebrow: I now choose to turn this around

Side of Eye: From now on I will trust my instincts

Under Eye: I will listen closely to my inner guidance

Under Nose: And I will not settle for less than I deserve

Chin: I am worthy of a loving, healthy relationship

Collarbone: I choose to allow love to flow into my life

Under Arm: I choose to be in alignment with what I want

Top of Head: I choose to believe I can achieve positive change

When your intensity level is below a 2, move on to the following script:

I Have a Bad Track Record

Karate Chop 3 Times:

Even though I have a bad track record, I choose to turn this around and allow love to flow into my life.

Round 1 (tapping through each point):

Even though I have a bad track record

Round 2 (tapping through each point):

I choose to turn this around and allow love to flow into my life

Round 3 (alternate while tapping through each point):

Even though I have a bad track record

I choose to turn this around and allow love to flow into my life

I HAVE A FEAR OF ABANDONMENT

Karate Chop: Even though I have a fear of abandonment, I choose to accept myself and my feelings.

Karate Chop: Even though I'm afraid I'll be abandoned, I choose to accept myself and my feelings.

Karate Chop: Even though I'm afraid I'll be left alone, I choose to accept myself and my feelings.

Round 1:

Eyebrow: I have a fear of abandonment

Side of Eye: I'm afraid I'll be left alone

Under Eye: It's hard for me to be trusting

Under Nose: I fear I'll be let down in the end

Chin: I feel so insecure

Collarbone: I'm afraid of being alone

Under Arm: I don't want to open my heart

Top of Head: Because I'm afraid I'll be hurt

Round 2:

Eyebrow: I don't know where this fear comes from

Side of Eye: I learned it from past experiences

Under Eye: I've been holding on to the fear for years

Under Nose: It's weighing me down

Chin: It's holding me back from a loving relationship

Collarbone: I want to let this fear go

Under Arm: I want to feel secure

Top of Head: I want to feel emotionally independent

Round 3:

Eyebrow: Maybe I can release this fear

Side of Eye: I'm so ready to let it go

Under Eye: I am open to healing my past

Under Nose: And moving forward as a stronger me

Chin: I now choose to let this fear go

Collarbone: I choose to feel safe and secure

Under Arm: I choose to be emotionally independent

Top of Head: I choose to be strong and empowered

When your intensity level is below a 2, move on to the following script:

I Have a Fear of Abandonment

Karate Chop 3 Times:

Even though I have a fear of abandonment, I choose to release the fear and become strong and empowered.

Round 1 (tapping through each point):

Even though I have a fear of abandonment

Round 2 (tapping through each point):

I choose to release the fear and become strong and empowered

Round 3 (alternate while tapping through each point):

Even though I have a fear of abandonment

I choose to release the fear and become strong and empowered

I HAVE A FEAR
OF INTIMACY

Karate Chop: Even though I have a fear of intimacy, I choose to love and accept myself anyway.

Karate Chop: Even though I'm afraid of intimacy, I choose to love and accept myself anyway.

Karate Chop: Even though I'm afraid to get close to someone, I choose to love and accept myself anyway.

Round 1:

Eyebrow: I am afraid of intimacy

Side of Eye: I fear getting too close to someone

Under Eye: I've had bad experiences in the past

Under Nose: So I feel a need to protect myself

Chin: I don't like being vulnerable

Collarbone: It's just too risky

Under Arm: I might get hurt again

Top of Head: It's safer to keep my distance

Round 2:

Eyebrow: I want to have a meaningful relationship

Side of Eye: I want to stop pushing people away

Under Eye: I want to release this fear of being hurt

Under Nose: I want to feel safe and secure

Chin: I want to open my heart to love again

Collarbone: Maybe I can let go of this fear

Under Arm: Maybe I can allow myself to heal from my past

Top of Head: Maybe I can feel safe in a relationship

Round 3:

Eyebrow: I now choose to open my heart to love again

Side of Eye: At my own pace and in my own time

Under Eye: I choose to nurture and support myself

Under Nose: I allow myself to heal from past experiences

Chin: I choose to allow an intimate connection with myself

Collarbone: And will allow another in when I'm ready

Under Arm: I choose to release my fear of being hurt

Top of Head: I choose to feel safe and secure

When your intensity level is below a 2, move on to the following script:

I Have a Fear of Intimacy

Karate Chop 3 Times:

Even though I have a fear of intimacy, I choose to release this fear and open my heart to a loving relationship.

Round 1 (tapping through each point):

Even though I have a fear of intimacy

Round 2 (tapping through each point):

I choose to release this fear and open my heart to a loving relationship

Round 3 (alternate while tapping through each point):

Even though I have a fear of intimacy

I choose to release this fear and open my heart to a loving relationship

I HAVE A FEAR OF REJECTION

Karate Chop: Even though I have a fear of rejection, I accept myself and how I feel.

Karate Chop: Even though I am afraid of rejection, I accept myself and how I feel.

Karate Chop: Even though I'm afraid I'll be rejected, I accept myself and how I feel.

Round 1:

Eyebrow: I have a fear of rejection

Side of Eye: I worry I won't be accepted

Under Eye: For who I am

Under Nose: Or what I believe

Chin: Or how I act

Collarbone: I fear disapproval

Under Arm: And lack of acceptance

Top of Head: I feel so inadequate

Round 2:

Eyebrow: I want to let go of this fear

Side of Eye: I want to feel accepted

Under Eye: I want to feel like I'm good enough

Under Nose: I want to be true to myself

Chin: I want to be authentic

Collarbone: I want to feel secure

Under Arm: I want to take back my power

Top of Head: I want to feel safe being who I am

Round 3:

Eyebrow: Maybe I can release this fear

Side of Eye: Maybe I can let it go

Under Eye: I don't have to be perfect

Under Nose: If I love who I am

Chin: Then maybe others will love me too

Collarbone: I choose to let go of this fear of rejection

Under Arm: I choose to accept myself as I am

Top of Head: My own acceptance is all that matters

When your intensity level is below a 2, move on to the following script:

I Have a Fear of Rejection

Karate Chop 3 Times:

Even though I have a fear of rejection, I choose to release this fear and be true to myself.

Round 1 (tapping through each point):

Even though I have a fear of rejection

Round 2 (tapping through each point):

I choose to release this fear and be true to myself

Round 3 (alternate while tapping through each point):

Even though I have a fear of rejection

I choose to release this fear and be true to myself

I HAVE A FEAR
OF BETRAYAL

Karate Chop: Even though I have a fear of betrayal, I accept myself and how I feel.

Karate Chop: Even though I'm afraid I'll be betrayed, I accept myself and how I feel.

Karate Chop: Even though I fear being betrayed, I accept myself and how I feel.

Round 1:

Eyebrow: I'm afraid of being betrayed

Side of Eye: It is one of my deepest fears

Under Eye: I am tormented with anxiety

Under Nose: I don't want to be hurt again

Chin: It seems impossible for me to trust

Collarbone: I battle the stronghold of negative thoughts

Under Arm: I am always on guard

Top of Head: I am so afraid of being betrayed

Round 2:

Eyebrow: I want to release the power this fear has over me

Side of Eye: I want to liberate myself from this anxiety

Under Eye: I want to let go of the past

Under Nose: I want to clear the pain and hurt

Chin: I want to forgive and move on

Collarbone: I want to renew my confidence and trust

Under Arm: I want to feel secure in a relationship

Top of Head: I want to feel lovable and worthy

Round 3:

Eyebrow: I now choose to release the pain of the past

Side of Eye: I choose to let go of the hurt of betrayal

Under Eye: I choose to take my power back

Under Nose: I choose to allow myself to trust again

Chin: I choose to experience my life to the fullest

Collarbone: I choose to make space for an amazing relationship

Under Arm: I choose to open my heart

Top of Head: And allow love to flow into my life

When your intensity level is below a 2, move on to the following script:

I Have a Fear of Betrayal

Karate Chop 3 Times:

Even though I have a fear of betrayal, I choose to take my power back and be open to love.

Round 1 (tapping through each point):

Even though I have a fear of betrayal

Round 2 (tapping through each point):

I choose to take my power back and be open to love

Round 3 (alternate while tapping through each point):

Even though I have a fear of betrayal

I choose to take my power back and be open to love

I'M AFRAID OF BEING CONTROLLED

Karate Chop: Even though I'm afraid of being controlled in a relationship, I choose to love and accept myself.

Karate Chop: Even though I have a fear of being controlled in a relationship, I choose to love and accept myself.

Karate Chop: Even though I'm afraid of not having control of my life in a relationship, I choose to love and accept myself.

Round 1:

Eyebrow: I'm afraid of being controlled in a relationship

Side of Eye: I don't feel strong enough to be my own person

Under Eye: I don't like confrontation or rocking the boat in any way

Under Nose: So I'm afraid I'll give up my personal control to my partner

Chin: I fear becoming too compliant or enabling

Collarbone: I fear becoming defensive, or living in denial

Under Arm: I fear withdrawal because I don't know how to be in control of my life

Top of Head: I fear becoming resentful and emotionally distant

Round 2:

Eyebrow: I want to release this fear

Side of Eye: I want to let go of this worry

Under Eye: I want to feel in control of my life

Under Nose: I want to find a partner who is kind and accepting

Chin: I want to find a partner who is my equal

Collarbone: I just want to be myself

Under Arm: I long for a healthy, fulfilling relationship

Top of Head: I want to feel strong and empowered

Round 3:

Eyebrow: I now choose to release this fear

Side of Eye: I choose to be strong and empowered

Under Eye: I choose to attract a healthy relationship

Under Nose: Where I can be myself

Chin: Where I can feel safe and loved

Collarbone: I can do anything I set my mind to

Under Arm: I choose to change this pattern within myself

Top of Head: I choose to be in control of my life

When your intensity level is below a 2, move on to the following script:

I'm Afraid of Being Controlled

Karate Chop 3 Times:

Even though I'm afraid of being controlled in a relationship, I choose to release this fear and be strong and empowered.

Round 1 (tapping through each point):

Even though I'm afraid of being controlled in a relationship

Round 2 (tapping through each point):

I choose to release this fear and be strong and empowered

Round 3 (alternate while tapping through each point):

Even though I'm afraid of being controlled in a relationship

I choose to release this fear and be strong and empowered

I'M AFRAID OF LOSING MY INDEPENDENCE

Karate Chop: Even though I'm afraid of losing my independence, I deeply and completely love and accept myself.

Karate Chop: Even though I fear losing my independence, I deeply and completely love and accept myself.

Karate Chop: Even though I don't want to give up my independence, I deeply and completely love and accept myself.

Round 1:

Eyebrow: I want to be in a relationship

Side of Eye: But I'm afraid of losing my independence

Under Eye: I'm afraid of losing my freedom

Under Nose: I don't want to have to compromise

Chin: I don't want to have to answer to someone else

Collarbone: I don't want someone telling me what I can and cannot do

Under Arm: It's hard being independent within a relationship

Top of Head: I don't want to give up my independence

Round 2:

Eyebrow: I really want to be in a loving relationship

Side of Eye: But I also want to be independent

Under Eye: I want to find a solution to this dilemma

Under Nose: Maybe I can have the best of both worlds

Chin: Maybe it's possible to be independent within a relationship

Collarbone: Maybe I can continue to make my own choices

Under Arm: Maybe I can find someone who shares this value

Top of Head: I get to choose who I settle down with

Round 3:

Eyebrow: I choose to be open to new possibilities

Side of Eye: I choose to attract someone who is perfect for me

Under Eye: I choose to attract someone who is compatible

Under Nose: I choose to attract someone who values freedom

Chin: I choose to attract someone who values independence

Collarbone: My intentions are powerful

Under Arm: I can have whatever I choose

Top of Head: I choose to have independence within a loving relationship

When your intensity level is below a 2, move on to the following script:

I'm Afraid of Losing My Independence

Karate Chop 3 Times:

Even though I'm afraid of losing my independence, I choose to release this fear and be open to attracting someone who shares my values.

Round 1 (tapping through each point):

Even though I'm afraid of losing my independence

Round 2 (tapping through each point):

I choose to release this fear and be open to attracting someone who shares my values

Round 3 (alternate while tapping through each point):

Even though I'm afraid of losing my independence

I choose to release this fear and be open to attracting someone who shares my values

I'M AFRAID I WILL ALWAYS BE ALONE

Karate Chop: Even though I'm afraid I will always be alone, I choose to accept my feelings and love myself anyway.

Karate Chop: Even though I worry that I will never find someone, I choose to accept my feelings and love myself anyway.

Karate Chop: Even though I have a fear that I will always be single, I choose to accept my feelings and love myself anyway.

Round 1:

Eyebrow: I'm afraid I will always be alone

Side of Eye: I worry that I will never find someone

Under Eye: Being single may be my destiny

Under Nose: I fear I won't find anyone who wants to be with me

Chin: I worry I'll never find someone to share my life with

Collarbone: I'm afraid I'll never find my soul mate

Under Arm: I'm scared there is no one out there for me

Top of Head: I feel so lonely for a companion

Round 2:

Eyebrow: I really want to be in a relationship

Side of Eye: I want to find my soul mate

Under Eye: I want to share my life with someone

Under Nose: I want to trade in this single life for a partner

Chin: But maybe it's not in the cards for me

Collarbone: Maybe I am destined to be single

Under Arm: Maybe I can learn to accept where I am

Top of Head: Maybe I can be happy with or without a partner

Round 3:

Eyebrow: I choose to look at this from a different angle

Side of Eye: Being single does have its advantages

Under Eye: There are lots of positive aspects about being on my own

Under Nose: Maybe I can embrace this time until a partner comes along

Chin: I can use this time to focus on being the best person I can be

Collarbone: I can love myself by indulging in what makes me happy

Under Arm: I choose to be strong and independent

Top of Head: I choose to be happy with or without a partner

When your intensity level is below a 2, move on to the following script:

I'm Afraid I Will Always Be Alone

Karate Chop 3 Times:

Even though I'm afraid I will always be alone, I choose to release the fear, accept where I am, and be happy anyway.

Round 1 (tapping through each point):

Even though I'm afraid I will always be alone

Round 2 (tapping through each point):

I choose to release the fear, accept where I am, and be happy anyway

Round 3 (alternate while tapping through each point):

Even though I'm afraid I will always be alone

I choose to release the fear, accept where I am, and be happy anyway

I'M AFRAID TO COMMIT TO A RELATIONSHIP

Karate Chop: Even though I'm afraid to commit to a relationship, I choose to accept myself and my feelings.

Karate Chop: Even though I'm afraid to make a commitment, I choose to accept myself and my feelings.

Karate Chop: Even though I have a fear of commitment, I choose to accept myself and my feelings.

Round 1:

Eyebrow: I'm afraid to commit to a relationship

Side of Eye: I'm afraid of losing my options

Under Eye: I'm afraid of being trapped

Under Nose: I'm afraid of losing myself

Chin: I'm afraid of repeating past mistakes

Collarbone: All of this fear around committing to a relationship

Under Arm: When my partner starts talking long term

Top of Head: All I can think of is how to escape

Round 2:

Eyebrow: I want to release this fear of commitment

Side of Eye: I want to release this quest for perfection

Under Eye: I want to release this fear of limitations

Under Nose: I want to release this fear of making more mistakes

Chin: I want to release this fear of losing my individuality

Collarbone: I want to learn to embrace my sense of self

Under Arm: I want to let go of the past and be open to new beginnings

Top of Head: I want to erase this fear of commitment

Round 3:

Eyebrow: I now choose to release all these fears that are holding me back

Side of Eye: I now choose to release all the false beliefs that have caused my fear

Under Eye: I choose to believe I can create my ideal relationship

Under Nose: I choose to believe I can retain my identity and sense of self

Chin: I choose to believe I can still feel free within a relationship

Collarbone: I choose to believe I can attract a partner who allows me to be myself

Under Arm: I choose to believe I can attract a partner who makes me feel safe

Top of Head: I choose to be open to the idea of a loving, committed relationship

When your intensity level is below a 2, move on to the following script:

I'm Afraid to Commit to a Relationship

Karate Chop 3 Times:

Even though I'm afraid to commit to a relationship, I choose to release these fears and be open to finding a loving partner who is perfect for me.

Round 1 (tapping through each point):

Even though I'm afraid to commit to a relationship

Round 2 (tapping through each point):

I choose to release these fears and be open to finding a loving partner who is perfect for me

Round 3 (alternate while tapping through each point):

Even though I'm afraid to commit to a relationship

I choose to release these fears and be open to finding a loving partner who is perfect for me

I'M TOO BUSY FOR
A RELATIONSHIP

Karate Chop: Even though I'm too busy for a relationship, I choose to love and accept myself anyway.

Karate Chop: Even though my life is too busy for a relationship, I choose to love and accept myself anyway.

Karate Chop: Even though I don't have time for a relationship, I choose to love and accept myself anyway.

Round 1:

Eyebrow: My life is so busy

Side of Eye: There's no time for a relationship

Under Eye: It's hard to meet people

Under Nose: When I'm working all the time

Chin: And if by chance I did meet someone

Collarbone: There would be no time for dating

Under Arm: I wish there were more hours in a day

Top of Head: So I could have enough time for a relationship

Round 2:

Eyebrow: My work/career is important to me

Side of Eye: But I also want to be in a relationship

Under Eye: Maybe I can find a way to include both

Under Nose: Maybe I can organize my time differently

Chin: Maybe I can learn to have a balanced life

Collarbone: It's my life and I get to choose how I spend my time

Under Arm: Maybe I just need to shift my thinking

Top of Head: Maybe I can create more time for love

Round 3:

Eyebrow: I choose to release this need to be so busy

Side of Eye: I choose to release the need to work so much

Under Eye: I choose to shift my thinking and priorities

Under Nose: I choose to balance my work and personal life

Chin: I choose to slow down and make time for a relationship

Collarbone: I choose to believe I can have the best of both worlds

Under Arm: I choose to believe that anything is possible

Top of Head: I choose to open my heart and schedule to allow someone special to come in

When your intensity level is below a 2, move on to the following script:

I'm Too Busy For a Relationship

Karate Chop 3 Times:

Even though I'm too busy for a relationship, I choose to be open to finding balance between my work and personal life.

Round 1 (tapping through each point):

Even though I'm too busy for a relationship

Round 2 (tapping through each point):

I choose to be open to finding balance between my work and personal life

Round 3 (alternate while tapping through each point):

Even though I'm too busy for a relationship

I choose to be open to finding balance between my work and personal life

I'M TOO INSECURE

Karate Chop: Even though I'm too insecure for a relationship, I accept myself as I am.

Karate Chop: Even though I feel too insecure to be in a relationship, I accept myself as I am.

Karate Chop: Even though my insecurity keeps me from having a healthy relationship, I accept myself as I am.

Round 1:

Eyebrow: I feel emotionally insecure

Side of Eye: It's been a problem in my relationships

Under Eye: I get uneasy and nervous

Under Nose: And perceive feelings of inadequacy

Chin: My insecurity drives men/women away

Collarbone: This problem was born from past pain and rejection

Under Arm: Now I tend to look for things to go wrong

Top of Head: All this insecurity is exhausting

Round 2:

Eyebrow: I want to release these paranoid feelings

Side of Eye: I want to stop analyzing everything

Under Eye: I want to learn to relax and be more confident

Under Nose: I want to feel good about myself

Chin: I want to be self-assured

Collarbone: I want to feel secure in who I am

Under Arm: I want to learn to be more trusting

Top of Head: I want to feel empowered

Round 3:

Eyebrow: I now choose to challenge my fears and insecurities

Side of Eye: I choose to stop being self-destructive

Under Eye: I choose to seek self-assurance

Under Nose: I choose to believe I am always okay

Chin: I choose to focus on the good

Collarbone: I choose to have a positive attitude

Under Arm: I choose to relax and be more confident

Top of Head: I choose to tap into the amazing person I really am

When your intensity level is below a 2, move on to the following script:

I'm Too Insecure

Karate Chop 3 Times:

Even though I'm too insecure for a relationship, I choose to relax and feel self-assured and secure.

Round 1 (tapping through each point):

Even though I'm too insecure for a relationship

Round 2 (tapping through each point):

I choose to relax and feel self-assured and secure

Round 3 (alternate while tapping through each point):

Even though I'm too insecure for a relationship

I choose to relax and feel self-assured and secure

I'M TOO NEEDY

Karate Chop: Even though I'm too needy in a relationship, I choose to accept myself anyway.

Karate Chop: Even though I'm too clingy in a relationship, I choose to accept myself anyway.

Karate Chop: Even though my neediness causes problems in my relationships, I choose to accept myself anyway.

Round 1:

Eyebrow: I'm too needy in my relationships

Side of Eye: It is an ongoing problem

Under Eye:I am too dependent and clingy

Under Nose: I tend to be possessive and jealous

Chin: I need continual reassurance

Collarbone: I have a hard time spending time on my own

Under Arm: The relationship becomes my life

Top of Head: I stop paying attention to my own needs

Round 2:

Eyebrow: I know it's an unattractive quality

Side of Eye: I want to release these feelings of self-doubt

Under Eye: I want to become more self-assured

Under Nose: I want to have emotional freedom

Chin: I want to feel more confident

Collarbone: I want to take responsibility for my feelings

Under Arm: I want to feel comfortable spending time on my own

Top of Head: I want to be able to take care of myself

Round 3:

Eyebrow: I now choose to release these feelings of insecurity

Side of Eye: I choose to release these feelings of self-doubt

Under Eye: I choose to work on building my self-esteem

Under Nose: I choose to be more balanced

Chin: I choose to be more confident

Collarbone: I choose to be more self-reliant

Under Arm: I choose to be more independent

Top of Head: I choose to relax and be myself

When your intensity level is below a 2, move on to the following script:

I'm Too Needy

Karate Chop 3 Times:

Even though I'm too needy in a relationship, I choose to relax and be more self-accepting.

Round 1 (tapping through each point):

Even though I'm too needy in a relationship

Round 2 (tapping through each point):

I choose to relax and be more self-accepting

Round 3 (alternate while tapping through each point):

Even though I'm too needy in a relationship

I choose to relax and be more self-accepting

I'M TOO SHY

Karate Chop: Even though I'm too shy, I choose to love and accept myself as I am.

Karate Chop: Even though I'm so shy, I choose to love and accept myself as I am.

Karate Chop: Even though I'm uncomfortable around people, I choose to love and accept myself as I am.

Round 1:

Eyebrow: I'm so bashful and shy

Side of Eye: It makes it hard to attract a relationship

Under Eye: I worry about what others think of me

Under Nose: I'm afraid I'll sound stupid so I keep quiet

Chin: I feel inadequate so I try to be invisible

Collarbone: I feel reserved and timid

Under Arm: I'm uncomfortable being seen or heard

Top of Head: I usually hope nobody will notice me

Round 2:

Eyebrow: I want to feel comfortable around people

Side of Eye: I want to feel at ease

Under Eye: I want to feel more confident

Under Nose: I want to relax and be myself

Chin: I want to feel good about who I am

Collarbone: Maybe it's possible to release this shyness

Under Arm: I wasn't born this way

Top of Head: Maybe I can regain my confidence

Round 3:

Eyebrow: I choose to release the belief that shyness is part of who I am

Side of Eye: I forgive anyone who ever tried to silence my voice

Under Eye: I choose to release the fear of rejection

Under Nose: I choose to release the feelings of inadequacy

Chin: I choose to release my doubt of self-worth

Collarbone: I choose to be relaxed and confident

Under Arm: I choose to believe I am a gift to this world

Top of Head: I choose to let the real me shine through

When your intensity level is below a 2, move on to the following script:

I'm Too Shy

Karate Chop 3 Times:

Even though I'm too shy, I choose to release these fears and allow the real me to shine through.

Round 1 (tapping through each point):

Even though I'm too shy

Round 2 (tapping through each point):

I choose to release these fears and allow the real me to shine through

Round 3 (alternate while tapping through each point):

Even though I'm too shy

I choose to release these fears and allow the real me to shine through

I FEEL UNATTRACTIVE

Karate Chop: Even though I feel unattractive, I choose to love and accept myself anyway.

Karate Chop: Even though I believe I'm unattractive, I choose to love and accept myself anyway.

Karate Chop: Even though I'm too unattractive, I choose to accept my feelings and who I am.

Round 1:

Eyebrow: I feel unattractive

Side of Eye: I feel ugly

Under Eye: I don't like the way I look

Under Nose: I am so conscious of my flaws

Chin: Some real, some imagined

Collarbone: I am so insecure

Under Arm: About my physical appearance

Top of Head: I feel too unattractive for love

Round 2:

Eyebrow: I want to feel better about myself

Side of Eye: I want to feel comfortable in my own skin

Under Eye: I want to accept myself as I am

Under Nose: I want to feel attractive

Chin: I want to feel beautiful

Collarbone: What if I am beautiful?

Under Arm: What if I am too critical of myself?

Top of Head: Beauty is in the eyes of the beholder

Round 3:

Eyebrow: I now choose to stop criticizing myself

Side of Eye: I choose to see myself as God/Spirit sees me

Under Eye: As a beautiful and radiant being

Under Nose: I choose to start by smiling more

Chin: And learning to love myself as I am

Collarbone: I choose to focus on my best qualities

Under Arm: I choose to believe that I can find love

Top of Head: I choose to be open to thinking I am attractive

When your intensity level is below a 2, move on to the following script:

I Feel Unattractive

Karate Chop 3 Times:

Even though I feel unattractive, I choose to stop criticizing myself and be open to thinking I'm attractive.

Round 1 (tapping through each point):

Even though I feel unattractive

Round 2 (tapping through each point):

I choose to stop criticizing myself and be open to thinking I'm attractive

Round 3 (alternate while tapping through each point):

Even though I feel unattractive

I choose to stop criticizing myself and be open to thinking I'm attractive

IT IS NOT SAFE FOR ANYONE TO LOVE ME

Karate Chop: Even though it is not safe for anyone to love me, I choose to accept myself and how I feel.

Karate Chop: Even though I don't want anyone to love me because it is not safe, I choose to accept myself and how I feel.

Karate Chop: Even though loving me is not safe, I choose to accept myself and how I feel.

Round 1:

Eyebrow: It is not safe for anyone to love me

Side of Eye: Because I don't know how to return love

Under Eye: I have shut down emotionally

Under Nose: To protect myself from pain

Chin: So if anyone tried to love me

Collarbone: They would feel my pain too

Under Arm: They would get hurt

Top of Head: Because I have nothing to offer

Round 2:

Eyebrow: I want to tear down this wall I have built around myself

Side of Eye: I want to allow love into my life

Under Eye: I want to open my heart

Under Nose: I want to know how to return love

Chin: Maybe I have conjured a false perception of myself

Collarbone: Maybe I'm just reacting from past experiences

Under Arm: Maybe I can heal from these wounds

Top of Head: Maybe I can open myself up to be loved

Round 3:

Eyebrow: I choose to release this belief that loving me is not safe

Side of Eye: I choose to begin releasing past hurts that are not serving me

Under Eye: I choose to open my heart and allow healing to take place

Under Nose: I choose to call on a higher power to guide me

Chin: I choose to be open to the possibility that I am worthy

Collarbone: I choose to be open to the possibility that I am lovable

Under Arm: I choose to start by loving myself

Top of Head: I choose to be open to the idea of allowing love to flow into my life

When your intensity level is below a 2, move on to the following script:

It is Not Safe For Anyone to Love Me

Karate Chop 3 Times:

Even though it is not safe for anyone to love me, I choose to love myself and be open to allowing love to flow into my life.

Round 1 (tapping through each point):

Even though it is not safe for anyone to love me

Round 2 (tapping through each point):

I choose to love myself and be open to allowing love to flow into my life

Round 3 (alternate while tapping through each point):

Even though it is not safe for anyone to love me

I choose to love myself and be open to allowing love to flow into my life

IT IS NOT SAFE FOR ME TO LOVE SOMEONE

Karate Chop: Even though it is not safe for me to love someone, I choose to accept myself and my feelings.

Karate Chop: Even though I don't feel safe opening my heart, I choose to accept myself and my feelings.

Karate Chop: Even though I'm afraid of being hurt, I choose to accept myself and my feelings.

Round 1:

Eyebrow: It's not safe for me to love someone

Side of Eye: The outcome is always the same

Under Eye: I open up and I give of myself

Under Nose: Only to be brokenhearted and/or betrayed

Chin: I've been hurt so many times in the past

Collarbone: I keep repeating the same old patterns

Under Arm: Now I'd rather play it safe

Top of Head: And not put myself in that position again

Round 2:

Eyebrow: I wish I could feel safe in a relationship

Side of Eye: I want to release these fears

Under Eye: I want to be able to open my heart

Under Nose: I want to experience lasting love

Chin: I want to feel valued and appreciated

Collarbone: I want to feel more secure

Under Arm: Maybe it is possible to break the cycle

Top of Head: I choose to be open to the possibility

Round 3:

Eyebrow: I am ready to change this pattern

Side of Eye: I am willing to face my fears

Under Eye: I am open to healing my heart

Under Nose: I am open to restoring my faith in love

Chin: I choose to release the past and move forward

Collarbone: I choose to have hope for my future

Under Arm: I choose to allow love to flow into my life

Top of Head: I choose to start by loving myself

When your intensity level is below a 2, move on to the following script:

It is Not Safe For Me to Love Someone

Karate Chop 3 Times:

Even though it is not safe for me to love someone, I choose to release my fears and allow love to flow into my life.

Round 1 (tapping through each point):

Even though it is not safe for me to love someone

Round 2 (tapping through each point):

I choose to release my fears and allow love to flow into my life

Round 3 (alternate while tapping through each point):

Even though it is not safe for me to love someone

I choose to release my fears and allow love to flow into my life

ABOUT THE AUTHOR

Christa Smith

Christa Smith is a Coach, EFT Practitioner and "Dream Life Mid-wife". She has a passion for personal and spiritual growth, and assisting others in creating their best life. Her coaching practice is based on the principles of conscious creation with a focus on vibration and energy management.

Christa is also a mom of 6 adult children and lives on the beautiful island of Maui.

Visit her website at www. Christa-Smith.com.

BOOKS BY THIS AUTHOR

Tapping Scripts For Weight Loss

Although EFT is simple to learn and apply, many find it challenging to formulate set-up statements and reminder phrases. This book has been created to take the guess work out of tapping by providing 52 EFT Tapping scripts that cover the most common weight loss obstacles, such as cravings, body image, emotions, exercise, food, forgiveness, and limiting beliefs.

Tapping Scripts For Money

Whether it's spending too much, never having enough, or being buried in debt, your thoughts, beliefs and emotions around money are the driving force behind your financial woes. When you are dealing with money problems, EFT (Emotional Freedom Technique) Tapping can help to release your stress and worry when you're facing money challenges, and set you on a path of emotional stability. Although EFT is simple to learn and apply, many find it challenging to formulate set-up statements and reminder phrases. This book has been created to take the guesswork out of tapping by providing 52 EFT Tapping scripts that cover the most common money issues. With EFT Tapping you can end your money struggles and literally tap your way to financial ease.

Tapping Scripts For Healing, Attracting & Finding Love

Whether you're recovering from a painful break-up, or are in search of a soul mate, EFT Tapping can help you release the internal blocks that prevent you from having the love you desire. Although EFT is simple to learn and apply, many find it challenging to formulate set-up statements and reminder phrases. This book has been created to take the guesswork out of tapping by providing 52 EFT Tapping scripts that cover the most common issues when you are looking for a relationship. With EFT Tapping you can end your struggles and literally tap your way to finding your soul mate.

Tapping Scripts For Nurturing, Maintaining & Keeping Love

While the early stages of a relationship can feel easy and exciting, successful long-term relationships can be challenging. Maintaining a healthy, happy, and satisfying partnership involves acceptance, open communication, and emotional stability. EFT (Emotional Freedom Technique) can help in all these crucial areas to keep your love connection strong and ongoing. Although EFT is simple to learn and apply, many find it challenging to formulate set-up statements and reminder phrases. This book has been created to take the guess work out of tapping by providing 52 EFT Tapping scripts that cover the most common relationship issues. With EFT Tapping you can release the negative emotions that compromise a healthy connection with your partner.

The Conscious Creator's Guide To Self-Coaching

Yes, you CAN be your own conscious creation coach! In fact, you can become the best coach you could possibly have. As a born creator, you already have within you everything you need to know to create your life as you want it to be. This program simply reminds you of this knowledge and gives you the tools and simple steps on how to apply it so that your dream life can become your reality.

The Conscious Creator's Guide To Meditation

Meditation is well known for its effectiveness in releasing stress from the mind and body, but is also the conscious creator's most valuable tool in developing a highly joyful, deeply fulfilling life. This book will help you to harness the power of meditation to enhance every area of your life and bring you into alignment with the powerful creator you were born to be.

The Conscious Creator's Guide To Winning The Lottery: A Law Of Attraction Game To Unlock Your Winning Potential

As born creators, we can be, do or have anything, and that includes winning the lottery. If you feel inspired to play, you have the potential to win. All it takes is aligning your energy with your dream.

This game was created to activate your imagination and raise your vibration so that you will be a match to increased financial abundance and potentially, a lottery winner. Keeping it in the context of a game, makes it fun and softens any resistance you might have around beliefs regarding the "statistics."

The truth is, it doesn't matter what the statistics are. If you align your energy, you can easily beat the odds and be a lottery jackpot winner. At the very least, this game will help you to expand your thinking, and your energy, so that you can move towards improved financial situations and live a more abundant life.

Law Of Attraction Quotes: From The Best Loa Teachers - Past And Present

This book is a collection of over 700 quotes from the best LOA teachers, past and present, including Abraham-Hicks, Catherine

Ponder, Ernest Holmes, Jack Canfield, Louise Hay, Mike Dooley, Napolean Hill, Wayne Dyer, and more. The wisdom from these inspiring leaders will empower and encourage you to live your very best life.

Manufactured by Amazon.ca
Bolton, ON

37824303R00059